Smart Selling: Harnessing AI for E-commerce Success

The Intelligent E- commerce Revolution

Zaytoona Nur

Table of Contents

Chapter 1 Introduction to AI in E-commerce.. 1

    The Evolution of E-commerce 1

    The Role of AI in Modern Retail 2

    Overview of AI Technologies in E-commerce 2

Chapter 2: AI-Driven Product Recommendation Systems.. 4

    Understanding Recommendation Algorithms 4

    Implementing AI Recommendations on E-commerce Platforms.................. 5

    Case Studies of Successful Implementations 6

Chapter 3: Chatbot Integration for Customer Service... 7

    The Importance of Customer Service in E-commerce................................. 7

    Designing Effective Chatbots for Online Retail 8

    Measuring the Impact of Chatbots on Customer Satisfaction 8

Chapter 4: Predictive Analytics for Inventory Management 10

    Fundamentals of Predictive Analytics 10

    Tools and Technologies for Inventory Management 11

    Best Practices for Implementing Predictive Analytics 12

Chapter 5: Personalised Marketing Strategies Using AI 13

    Creating Customer Pro les with AI 13

    Targeted Marketing Campaigns.. 14

    Evaluating the Effectiveness of Personalised Marketing 14

Chapter 6: AI-Based Pricing Optimisation Tools 16

    The Science Behind Pricing Strategies 16

    AI Tools for Dynamic Pricing.. 17

    Case Studies on Pricing Optimisation.. 17

Chapter 7: AI-Enhanced Supply Chain Logistics... 19

    Understanding Supply Chain Challenges in E-commerce.......................... 19

    AI Solutions for Streamlining Logistics 20

The Future of AI in Supply Chain Management 20

Chapter 8: Voice Commerce and AI Assistants 22

The Rise of Voice Commerce 22

Integrating AI Assistants into E-commerce Platforms 23

Enhancing User Experience Through Voice Interaction 23

Chapter 9: User Behaviour Analysis Using AI 25

Techniques for Analysing User Behaviour 25

Tools for Enhancing E-commerce UX Design 26

Leveraging Data for Continuous Improvement 26

Chapter 10: Future Trends in AI and E-commerce 28

Emerging Technologies to Watch 28

The Impact of AI on E-commerce Strategies 29

Preparing for the Future of Retail with AI 29

Chapter 1

Introduction to AI in E-commerce

The Evolution of E-commerce

The evolution of e-commerce has been a remarkable journey, reflecting the rapid technological advancements and shifting consumer behaviours over the last few decades. Initially, e-commerce emerged as a concept in the 1960s with the introduction of Electronic Data Interchange (EDI), allowing businesses to exchange documents electronically. However, it was not until the advent of the internet in the 1990s that e-commerce began to flourish, leading to the establishment of online marketplaces like Amazon and eBay. These platforms set the foundation for a new era of retail, where convenience and accessibility became paramount for consumers.

As technology advanced, so did the capabilities of e-commerce platforms. The integration of artificial intelligence (AI) marked a significant turning point in this evolution. AI-driven product recommendation systems began to transform the shopping experience by analysing customer data to suggest personalised products based on individual preferences and behaviours. This personalisation not only enhanced user satisfaction but also increased conversion rates, illustrating the powerful impact of AI on e-commerce success. As students and professionals in the e-commerce field, understanding these developments is crucial for leveraging AI to create compelling shopping experiences.

The rise of chatbots in customer service has also played a pivotal role in the evolution of e-commerce. These AI-driven virtual assistants provide instant support to customers, answering queries and guiding them through the purchasing process. By automating customer interactions, businesses can deliver 24/7 support, improve response times, and enhance overall customer satisfaction. For newcomers to the e- commerce industry, integrating chatbots into their platforms can be a game-changer, allowing them to focus on other critical aspects of their operations while maintaining high levels of customer engagement.

Predictive analytics has further revolutionised inventory management and marketing strategies in e-commerce. By analysing historical data and consumer trends, businesses can forecast demand more accurately, optimise stock levels, and reduce waste. This data-driven approach not only leads to cost savings but also ensures that customers and the products they want when they want them. Additionally, AI algorithms enable personalised marketing strategies, allowing businesses to target specific customer segments with tailored messages, thereby increasing the effectiveness of their marketing campaigns.

Lastly, the ongoing development of voice commerce and AI assistants is reshaping how consumers interact with e- commerce platforms. Voice-activated shopping has gained traction, providing a hands-free and convenient way for customers to browse and make purchases. Coupled with AI-enhanced supply chain logistics and user behaviour analysis, e-commerce businesses can refine their user experience (UX) designs to create seamless shopping experiences. As the landscape of e-commerce continues to evolve, staying informed about these advancements is essential for anyone looking to thrive in this dynamic field.

The Role of AI in Modern Retail

The integration of artificial intelligence (AI) in modern retail has revolutionised how businesses operate and interact with consumers. In the realm of e-commerce, AI- driven technologies are becoming essential tools for enhancing customer experiences and optimising operations. From personalised product recommendations to advanced customer service chatbots, AI is reshaping the landscape of online retail.

Understanding the various applications of AI in this sector is crucial for students and professionals aiming to thrive in the competitive e-commerce environment.

One of the most impactful uses of AI in e-commerce is through product recommendation systems. These algorithms analyse user behaviour and preferences to suggest products tailored to individual customers. By leveraging data from past purchases, browsing history, and demographic information, AI can significantly enhance the shopping experience. This level of personalisation not only increases customer satisfaction but also drives sales, as shoppers are more likely to purchase items that align with their interests. For newcomers to the field, mastering the fundamentals of AI-driven recommendations can set the foundation for a successful career in e-commerce.

Another significant application of AI in retail is the integration of chatbots for customer service. These AI-powered tools can handle inquiries, assist with order tracking, and provide product information around the clock. By automating customer interactions, businesses can improve response times and reduce operational costs. For students and professionals, understanding how to implement and optimise chatbot technology can enhance customer engagement and retention, key components in building a successful online brand.

Predictive analytics is another critical area where AI plays a vital role in inventory management. By analysing historical sales data and market trends, AI tools can forecast demand for products, helping retailers maintain optimal stock levels. This capability not only minimises the risks of overstocking or stockouts but also allows businesses to make informed decisions about their supply chain logistics. For those setting up their e-commerce ventures, leveraging AI for predictive analytics can lead to more efficient operations and a better overall customer experience.

Lastly, AI enhances personalised marketing strategies, ensuring that businesses can target their customers effectively. By utilising AI algorithms, retailers can segment their audience and deliver tailored marketing messages that resonate with specific consumer groups. This precision in targeting increases the likelihood of conversion and fosters brand loyalty. Additionally, AI-based pricing optimisation tools allow businesses to adjust their pricing strategies dynamically based on market conditions and competitor actions, further improving profitability. As the e-commerce landscape continues to evolve, understanding these AI applications will be crucial for anyone looking to succeed in this dynamic field.

Overview of AI Technologies in E-commerce

The integration of artificial intelligence (AI) technologies in e-commerce is transforming the landscape of online retail, offering innovative solutions that enhance operational efficiency and customer experience. From personalised shopping experiences to smarter inventory management, AI is becoming an essential component for businesses seeking to thrive in a competitive market. E-commerce students and professionals must understand the various AI applications that are shaping the industry, as these technologies not only streamline processes but also create opportunities for differentiation.

Smart Selling: Harnessing AI for E-commerce Success

One of the most notable applications of AI in e-commerce is the use of AI-driven product recommendation systems. These systems analyse customer behaviour, preferences, and purchase history to suggest relevant products, ultimately increasing conversion rates and enhancing customer satisfaction. By leveraging machine learning algorithms, e-commerce platforms can deliver personalised recommendations that resonate with individual users, fostering a more engaging shopping experience. This technology not only drives sales but also builds customer loyalty, making it a vital tool for any online retailer.

Chatbot integration has emerged as a significant trend in customer service for online retail. AI-powered chatbots provide instant support to customers, addressing inquiries and resolving issues 24/7. They can handle a wide range of tasks, from answering frequently asked questions to guiding users through complex purchasing processes. By employing natural language processing, these chatbots can understand and respond to customer queries in real time, enhancing user satisfaction and reducing the workload for human customer service representatives. As e-commerce continues to grow, the role of chatbots in maintaining high levels of customer engagement will only increase.

Predictive analytics is another crucial AI technology that aids in inventory management within e-commerce. By analysing historical sales data, market trends, and customer purchasing patterns, businesses can forecast demand more accurately. This predictive capability helps retailers optimise their stock levels, reducing the risk of overstocking or stockouts. Implementing predictive analytics not only enhances operational efficiency but also ensures that customers find the products they want and are available when they need them, thereby improving overall customer experience.

AI also plays a vital role in personalised marketing strategies and pricing optimisation for e-commerce businesses. By utilising algorithms that analyse customer data, retailers can tailor marketing campaigns to target specific demographics effectively. Furthermore, AI-based pricing optimisation tools allow businesses to adjust prices dynamically based on factors such as competitor pricing, demand fluctuations, and customer behaviour. This strategic use of AI enables e-commerce companies to remain competitive and maximise profitability while ensuring that customers receive fair pricing. As these technologies continue to evolve, understanding their implications will be critical for anyone involved in the e-commerce sector.

Chapter 2

AI-Driven Product Recommendation Systems

Understanding Recommendation Algorithms

Understanding recommendation algorithms is crucial for anyone involved in e-commerce, as these systems are integral to enhancing customer experience and driving sales. At their core, recommendation algorithms analyse user data to suggest products that align with individual preferences and behaviours. This data can come from various sources, including past purchases, browsing history, and even customer ratings. By leveraging these insights, e-commerce platforms can deliver personalised shopping experiences that not only increase conversion rates but also foster customer loyalty.

There are several types of recommendation algorithms, each utilising distinct methodologies to predict what users might want. Collaborative filtering is one of the most common approaches, which relies on the behaviour of similar users to make suggestions. For example, if User A and User B have similar purchase histories, the algorithm may recommend products that User B has purchased to User A. Content- based filtering, on the other hand, focuses on the characteristics of the products themselves, suggesting items based on similarities in features, categories, or descriptions. Understanding these methods is essential for e-commerce professionals looking to implement effective recommendation systems.

Integrating recommendation algorithms into an e-commerce platform can significantly enhance user engagement. By offering personalised product suggestions, businesses can create a tailored shopping experience that encourages customers to explore more items and ultimately increase their average order value. Moreover, these algorithms can adapt and evolve over time, learning from new data inputs to refine their suggestions. This adaptability is particularly beneficial in a fast-paced e-commerce landscape, where consumer preferences can shift rapidly.

In addition to product recommendations, AI-driven systems can also optimise customer interactions through chatbots. These AI assistants can utilise recommendation algorithms to provide real-time suggestions based on user queries or common purchase patterns. By integrating chatbots into customer service, e-commerce platforms can streamline the shopping experience, addressing customer needs more efficiently and enhancing satisfaction. This synergy between recommendation algorithms and chatbot technology exemplifies the potential of AI to transform online retail.

Lastly, the implementation of recommendation algorithms can extend beyond user-facing features to impact inventory management and supply chain logistics. Predictive analytics powered by these algorithms can help businesses forecast demand for specific products, enabling more efficient inventory management. This ensures that popular items are always in stock while minimising overstock of less desirable products. By understanding the full scope of recommendation algorithms and their applications, e-commerce professionals can harness AI to drive success across multiple facets of their business.

Implementing AI Recommendations on E-commerce Platforms

Implementing AI recommendations on e-commerce platforms is pivotal in modern retail strategies, primarily due to the increasing demand for personalised shopping experiences. E-commerce platforms can leverage AI-driven product recommendation systems to analyse vast amounts of consumer data, including browsing habits, purchase history, and demographic information. By employing machine learning algorithms, these systems can predict what products a customer is likely to be interested in, thus enhancing the overall shopping experience. This personalised approach not only improves customer satisfaction but also significantly boosts conversion rates, as consumers are more inclined to purchase items that resonate with their individual preferences.

Integrating chatbots into customer service frameworks is another crucial aspect of implementing AI recommendations. Chatbots utilise natural language processing to provide immediate assistance, answer queries, and guide customers through their shopping journey. By analysing user interactions, chatbots can suggest products, recommend alternatives, and even provide upsell opportunities based on previous purchases. This seamless integration of AI-driven customer service not only enhances user engagement but also frees up human resources to focus on more complex inquiries, leading to a more efficient operational model.

Predictive analytics plays a vital role in inventory management for e-commerce businesses. By analysing historical sales data and market trends, AI algorithms can forecast inventory needs, helping retailers maintain optimal stock levels. This not only reduces the risk of overstocking or stockouts but also aligns product availability with consumer demand. Effective inventory management ensures that popular items are always in stock, enhancing the customer experience and maximising sales potential. Moreover, it allows businesses to respond swiftly to market fluctuations, ultimately contributing to a more resilient supply chain.

Personalised marketing strategies powered by AI algorithms can significantly enhance the effectiveness of e-commerce promotions. By utilising data analytics to segment customers based on their behaviour and preferences, businesses can tailor marketing campaigns to specific audiences. This level of personalisation increases the relevance of advertisements and promotional offers, leading to higher engagement rates and improved customer loyalty. Furthermore, AI can optimise pricing strategies based on competitive analysis and consumer demand, ensuring that businesses remain attractive while maximising profit margins.

Finally, understanding user behaviour through AI analysis is essential for enhancing the user experience (UX) design of e-commerce platforms. By tracking how customers navigate through websites, which products they view, and where they drop off in the buying process, businesses can identify pain points and opportunities for improvement. This data-driven approach allows for informed design decisions that create a more intuitive and satisfying shopping environment. As e-commerce continues to evolve, the integration of AI not only streamlines operations but also fundamentally transforms how businesses interact with consumers, making it essential for aspiring e-commerce professionals to harness these technologies effectively.

Case Studies of Successful Implementations

In the realm of e-commerce, numerous businesses have successfully integrated artificial intelligence (AI) to enhance their operations and customer experiences. One notable case study is Amazon, which has leveraged AI-driven product recommendation systems to significantly boost sales. By analysing user behaviour, purchase history, and preferences, Amazon's algorithms generate personalised recommendations for shoppers. This approach not only improves the shopping experience but also increases conversion rates, leading to higher revenue. Students and professionals in e-commerce can learn from Amazon's model, as it illustrates the power of data-driven decisions in shaping consumer interactions.

Another compelling example is Sephora, which has effectively utilised AI chatbots to enhance customer service. Through its Virtual Artist tool, Sephora enables customers to try on makeup virtually by using augmented reality technology. This integration of AI not only engages customers but also provides them with personalised product suggestions based on their preferences and skin tones. The success of Sephora's chatbot integration showcases how AI can streamline customer interactions, reduce response times, and ultimately foster brand loyalty. E-commerce newcomers can draw valuable insights from this case, as it highlights the importance of innovation in customer engagement strategies.

Walmart serves as a prime example of predictive analytics in inventory management. The retail giant employs AI algorithms to forecast demand and optimise stock levels, ensuring that products are available when customers need them. By analysing sales trends, seasonal fluctuations, and market conditions, Walmart enhances its supply chain efficiency, reducing costs and minimising stockouts. For those entering the e-commerce field, Walmart's practices emphasise the critical role of predictive analytics in maintaining operational effectiveness and customer satisfaction, illustrating how AI can transform traditional inventory management into a more responsive system.

Personalised marketing strategies have also gained traction among e-commerce businesses, with Netflix leading the way in content recommendations. By analysing user viewing habits and preferences, Netflix delivers tailored content suggestions that keep subscribers engaged and reduce churn. This approach demonstrates the effectiveness of AI algorithms in creating personalised marketing campaigns that resonate with individual customers. E-commerce professionals can learn from Netflix's strategy to enhance their own marketing efforts, emphasising the significance of personalisation in driving customer loyalty and increasing sales.

Lastly, companies like Stitch Fix have successfully implemented AI-based pricing optimisation tools to stay competitive in the market. By analysing data on consumer behaviour, market trends, and competitor pricing, Stitch Fix dynamically adjusts its prices to maximise profitability while remaining attractive to customers. This application of AI in pricing strategies illustrates the potential for e-commerce businesses to utilise data analytics for informed decision-making. For students and professionals, Stitch Fix's approach serves as a vital lesson on the importance of agile pricing strategies in an ever-evolving e-commerce landscape, underscoring how AI can be harnessed to achieve strategic business objectives.

Chapter 3

Chatbot Integration for Customer Service

The Importance of Customer Service in E-commerce

Customer service plays a pivotal role in the e-commerce landscape, acting as a bridge between businesses and consumers. In an environment where competition is fierce and options are plentiful, the quality of customer service can significantly influence purchasing decisions and customer loyalty. E-commerce students and professionals must understand that effective customer service extends beyond traditional interactions; it encompasses the entire shopping experience, from the first click to post-purchase support. In a digitally-driven market, where immediacy is expected, the ability to provide excellent customer service can differentiate a brand and foster long-term relationships with customers.

AI technologies have revolutionised customer service in e-commerce, enabling businesses to offer personalised and efficient support. Chatbots, for instance, have become essential tools that facilitate instant communication, addressing customer inquiries 24/7. These AI-driven solutions not only enhance responsiveness but also streamline operations by handling routine questions, allowing human agents to focus on more complex issues. Understanding how to leverage chatbot integration effectively is crucial for newcomers in the e-commerce field, as it can lead to improved customer satisfaction and retention rates.

Moreover, predictive analytics plays a significant role in inventory management, which is directly tied to customer service. By analysing user behaviour and purchasing patterns, businesses can anticipate demand and ensure that popular products are always in stock. This proactive approach minimises the chances of stockouts, which can lead to customer frustration and lost sales. E-commerce professionals must recognise the importance of integrating predictive analytics into their operational strategies to enhance service quality and meet customer expectations.

Personalised marketing strategies powered by AI algorithms further enhance customer service by ensuring that communications and offers are relevant to individual consumers. By analysing customer data, businesses can tailor their marketing efforts, presenting the right products at the right time. This personalised experience not only increases conversion rates but also builds a sense of connection between the brand and the customer. E-commerce students should explore how these strategies can be implemented to create a more engaging and customer-centric shopping experience.

Finally, the evolving landscape of e-commerce necessitates an understanding of user experience (UX) design and its impact on customer service. AI-driven tools that analyse user behaviour can uncover insights that inform website design, navigation, and overall functionality. By prioritising user experience, businesses can create seamless interactions that foster customer loyalty. E-commerce professionals must continuously adapt to changing consumer expectations and leverage AI to enhance the overall shopping experience, recognising that exceptional customer service is integral to achieving success in the online retail space.

Designing Effective Chatbots for Online Retail

Designing effective chatbots for online retail involves a strategic approach that marries technology with customer service principles. At the core of this process is understanding the customer journey and identifying key touchpoints where a chatbot can enhance the shopping experience. Chatbots should be designed to provide immediate responses to customer inquiries, assist in product discovery, and streamline the checkout process. To achieve this, it is essential to map out common customer queries and interactions, ensuring that the chatbot is equipped with the necessary information and functionalities to address these effectively.

The design of the chatbot interface plays a crucial role in user engagement. A clean, intuitive interface encourages interaction and makes it easier for customers to navigate the chatbot's capabilities. Incorporating elements such as quick reply buttons, visual product recommendations, and personalised greetings can significantly enhance user experience. The chatbot should also maintain a consistent brand voice, which helps in fostering trust and familiarity among users. By integrating AI-driven product recommendation systems, chatbots can offer personalised suggestions based on user preferences and past interactions, thereby increasing the likelihood of conversions.

Integration of chatbots with existing customer service channels is vital for a seamless experience. Chatbots should not operate in isolation but rather complement human agents by handling routine inquiries and escalating more complex issues to human representatives. This hybrid approach ensures that customers receive timely assistance while allowing human agents to focus on higher-value interactions.

Additionally, leveraging predictive analytics can help chatbots anticipate customer needs, providing proactive support and enhancing the overall shopping experience.

To ensure the effectiveness of chatbots, continuous monitoring and optimisation are necessary. Analysing user interactions can reveal insights into common pain points and areas for improvement. Metrics such as response time, resolution rates, and customer satisfaction scores provide valuable feedback on the chatbot's performance. Regular updates and training of the chatbot's AI algorithms can help adapt to evolving customer preferences and behaviours, ensuring the technology remains relevant and effective.

Finally, embracing emerging technologies such as voice commerce can further enhance the capabilities of chatbots in online retail. By enabling voice-activated interactions, retailers can cater to a growing segment of consumers who prefer hands-free shopping experiences. This approach not only enhances accessibility but also aligns with the increasing trend of using AI assistants in everyday life. By designing chatbots that leverage voice recognition and natural language processing, e-commerce businesses can create a more engaging and personalised shopping journey that resonates with modern consumers.

Measuring the Impact of Chatbots on Customer Satisfaction

Measuring the impact of chatbots on customer satisfaction is crucial for e-commerce businesses looking to enhance their customer service experience. As the digital marketplace becomes increasingly competitive, understanding how chatbots influence customer interactions can help businesses optimise their operations. Chatbots serve as virtual assistants that can engage customers in real-time, providing immediate responses to inquiries. This immediacy can significantly enhance customer satisfaction by reducing wait times and ensuring that support is available 24/7. By analysing customer feedback and satisfaction scores pre- and post-chatbot implementation, businesses can quantify the improvements in user experience.

One key metric for assessing the impact of chatbots is the Net Promoter Score (NPS). This measure evaluates customer loyalty and their likelihood of recommending a service or product to others. By comparing NPS ratings before and after the chatbot deployment, e-commerce companies can gain insights into how these tools influence customer perceptions. A higher NPS after integrating chatbots typically indicates that customers appreciate the quick responses and support they receive, highlighting the chatbot's role in enhancing overall satisfaction. Additionally, businesses can track customer retention rates to further understand the long-term effects of chatbot interactions on loyalty.

Another important aspect of measuring chatbot effectiveness is analysing customer engagement metrics. These include the frequency of interactions, the average duration of chatbot conversations, and the rate of successful resolutions. By employing analytics tools, e-commerce platforms can gauge how often customers engage with the chatbot and whether their issues are resolved satisfactorily. High engagement rates coupled with successful resolution metrics suggest that customers find the chatbot helpful and responsive. Conversely, if engagement is low or resolution rates are unsatisfactory, this signals a need for improvement in the chatbot's performance.

Feedback mechanisms play a vital role in assessing chatbot impact. Implementing post-interaction surveys can provide direct insights into customer sentiments regarding their chatbot experiences. Questions can focus on the clarity of responses, the helpfulness of the information provided, and overall satisfaction with the interaction. This qualitative data complements quantitative metrics, allowing businesses to identify specific areas for enhancement. Moreover, analysing common customer inquiries can inform chatbot training, ensuring that the virtual assistant evolves to meet customer needs effectively.

In conclusion, measuring the impact of chatbots on customer satisfaction is multifaceted and requires a combination of quantitative and qualitative approaches. By leveraging metrics such as NPS, customer engagement rates, and direct feedback, e-commerce businesses can gain a comprehensive understanding of how chatbots enhance the customer experience. This analysis not only aids in enhancing chatbot performance but also aligns with broader marketing strategies, such as personalised marketing and predictive analytics. As e-commerce continues to evolve, the effective integration of AI-driven tools like chatbots will be pivotal in maintaining customer satisfaction and driving business success.

Chapter 4

Predictive Analytics for Inventory Management

Fundamentals of Predictive Analytics

Predictive analytics serves as a cornerstone for modern e-commerce, enabling businesses to anticipate future trends and make informed decisions. At its core, predictive analytics involves the use of statistical algorithms and machine learning techniques to analyse historical data and identify patterns. By leveraging these insights, e-commerce platforms can optimise various facets of their operations, from inventory management to personalised marketing strategies. Understanding the fundamentals of predictive analytics is essential for e-commerce students and professionals aiming to harness its power for enhanced business performance.

One of the primary applications of predictive analytics in e-commerce is AI-driven product recommendation systems. These systems analyse customer behaviour and preferences to suggest products that are likely to resonate with individual users. By utilising data such as previous purchases, browsing history, and demographic information, e-commerce platforms can create a tailored shopping experience that not only boosts conversion rates but also enhances customer satisfaction. The ability to predict which products a customer might be interested in fosters a sense of personalisation, making the shopping experience feel more intuitive and engaging.

Another critical area where predictive analytics shines is in inventory management. E- commerce businesses face the challenge of maintaining optimal stock levels to meet customer demand without overstocking, which ties up capital and increases storage costs. By applying predictive analytics, businesses can forecast demand based on historical sales data, seasonal trends, and market fluctuations. This allows for more accurate inventory planning, ensuring that products are available when customers want them while minimising excess stock. As a result, e-commerce companies can improve their operational efficiency and reduce costs associated with inventory mismanagement.

Predictive analytics also plays a vital role in shaping personalised marketing strategies. By analysing user behaviour and preferences, e-commerce platforms can segment their audience and deliver targeted marketing campaigns. These campaigns can include tailored email marketing, personalised discounts, and dynamic pricing strategies. Utilising AI algorithms to predict customer responses enables businesses to allocate resources efficiently, focusing on high-potential leads and increasing return on investment. This level of personalisation not only drives sales but also cultivates brand loyalty among customers.

Lastly, the integration of predictive analytics in customer service, particularly through chatbots, enhances the online shopping experience by providing timely support and information. Chatbots equipped with predictive capabilities can anticipate customer inquiries based on previous interactions and common queries. This proactive approach not only improves response times but also enhances user engagement. By understanding customer behaviour patterns, businesses can further review their service offerings, ensuring that customers receive relevant assistance promptly. As e- commerce continues to evolve, the mastery of predictive analytics will be crucial for students and professionals seeking to thrive in this dynamic landscape.

Tools and Technologies for Inventory Management

In the rapidly evolving world of e-commerce, effective inventory management is essential for success. With the integration of advanced tools and technologies, businesses can streamline their operations, minimise costs, and enhance customer satisfaction. Inventory management systems powered by artificial intelligence (AI) are at the forefront of these advancements, offering solutions that adapt to the dynamic demands of the market. These tools enable e-commerce businesses to predict inventory needs, manage stock levels, and optimise storage, ensuring that products are available when customers need them.

AI-driven product recommendation systems play a crucial role in inventory management by analysing user behaviour and preferences. By utilising machine learning algorithms, these systems can identify trends in customer purchasing behaviour, allowing businesses to adjust their inventory accordingly. For example, if data shows a surge in demand for a particular product, e-commerce platforms can proactively increase stock levels to meet customer expectations. This not only enhances the shopping experience but also reduces the risk of overstocking or stockouts, which can significantly impact sales and customer loyalty.

Chatbot integration for customer service further enhances inventory management strategies. Chatbots can provide real-time information about product availability, helping customers make informed purchasing decisions. When integrated with the inventory management system, chatbots can access up-to-date stock levels and notify customers about product restocks or alternative options if items are unavailable. This seamless communication fosters a positive customer experience, as shoppers feel informed and supported throughout their purchasing journey.

Predictive analytics is another powerful tool that e-commerce businesses can leverage for effective inventory management. By analysing historical sales data, market trends, and external factors such as seasonality or economic shifts, predictive analytics can forecast future inventory needs with remarkable accuracy. This foresight allows businesses to make informed decisions about ordering and stocking, reducing excess inventory costs and minimising waste. Implementing predictive analytics not only optimises inventory levels but also enhances supply chain logistics, ensuring that products are delivered efficiently to meet customer demands.

In addition to these technologies, AI-based pricing optimisation tools are vital for e-commerce inventory management. These tools analyse various factors, including competitor pricing, customer behaviour, and market trends, to suggest optimal pricing strategies that maximise revenue. By adjusting prices in real-time based on demand fluctuations and inventory levels, e-commerce businesses can remain competitive while ensuring they are not missing out on potential profits. Ultimately, the integration of these tools and technologies not only streamlines inventory management processes but also supports broader marketing strategies, creating a cohesive and responsive e-commerce environment that meets the needs of both businesses and consumers alike.

Best Practices for Implementing Predictive Analytics

To successfully implement predictive analytics in e-commerce, businesses must first prioritise data quality. This begins with ensuring that data collected from various sources, such as customer interactions, sales transactions, and website analytics, is accurate, complete, and relevant. E-commerce platforms should invest in data cleansing practices to eliminate inaccuracies and redundancies. Additionally, establishing a robust data governance framework will help maintain data integrity over time. High-quality data is the cornerstone of effective predictive analytics, as it ensures that insights drawn from the data are reliable and actionable.

Next, e-commerce businesses should focus on selecting the right predictive analytics tools that align with their specific needs and objectives. With a myriad of options available in the market, it is crucial to assess features that cater to unique business requirements, such as AI-driven product recommendation systems or AI-based pricing optimisation tools. Organisations should evaluate the scalability of these tools to accommodate future growth and the potential integration capabilities with existing systems, including customer relationship management (CRM) software and inventory management platforms. A well-chosen tool can significantly enhance the effectiveness of predictive analytics initiatives.

Training and development of staff are vital components for implementing predictive analytics successfully. E-commerce businesses should invest in training programs that equip employees with the necessary skills to interpret data insights and apply them to their daily operations. This includes understanding AI algorithms, user behaviour analysis, and the implications of predictive modelling on marketing strategies. By fostering a data-driven culture, organisations empower their teams to leverage analytics for informed decision-making, enhancing the overall effectiveness of marketing campaigns and inventory management practices.

Another best practice involves continuous monitoring and evaluation of predictive analytics outcomes. Businesses should establish key performance indicators (KPIs) to assess the impact of predictive analytics on various aspects of their operations, such as customer engagement, sales growth, and inventory turnover rates. Regular reviews of these metrics allow companies to refine their predictive models and adjust their strategies accordingly. This iterative process ensures that predictive analytics remains relevant and effective in an ever-evolving e-commerce landscape.

Lastly, fostering collaboration between departments is essential for maximising the benefits of predictive analytics. E-commerce organisations should encourage cross-functional teams to share insights and strategies derived from predictive analytics, bridging gaps between marketing, customer service, inventory management, and supply chain logistics. By aligning efforts across departments, businesses can create a cohesive approach that enhances the customer experience, optimises inventory, and ultimately drives sales. Integrating predictive analytics into the fabric of e-commerce operations not only improves efficiency but also positions companies to better anticipate market trends and customer needs.

Chapter 5

Personalised Marketing Strategies Using AI

Creating Customer Profiles with AI

Creating customer profiles with AI is a transformative step for e-commerce businesses aiming to enhance user experiences and optimise marketing strategies. At the core of this process lies the ability to gather and analyse vast amounts of data from various customer interactions. E-commerce platforms can leverage AI algorithms to process information obtained from user behaviours, transaction histories, and demographic data. By synthesising this data into comprehensive customer profiles, businesses can gain insights into their target audience's preferences, shopping habits, and pain points, allowing for more tailored marketing approaches.

One of the primary benefits of AI-driven customer profiling is the ability to segment customers based on their behaviours and preferences. Traditional methods of customer segmentation often rely on broad demographic factors, which can overlook the nuances of individual shopping behaviours. AI enables e-commerce platforms to create dynamic segments that evolve as customer behaviours change. This adaptability ensures that marketing strategies remain relevant and effective, allowing businesses to engage with customers in a more personalised manner, ultimately driving higher conversion rates and customer loyalty.

In addition to segmentation, AI enhances the accuracy of predictive analytics, which is essential for anticipating future customer needs. By analysing historical data, AI algorithms can forecast trends in customer behaviour, such as predicting which products a customer is likely to purchase next. This capability is not only useful for recommending products through AI-driven recommendation systems but also plays a crucial role in inventory management. Understanding potential customer demand can help e-commerce businesses optimise their stock levels, reducing excess inventory and improving cash flow.

Chatbot integration further amplifies the effectiveness of customer profiling. AI-powered chatbots can engage with customers in real-time, gathering additional data through conversations while providing immediate assistance. This interaction not only enhances the customer service experience but also contributes to the richness of customer profiles. By analysing chat logs and customer queries, businesses can refine their understanding of customer needs and preferences, leading to more effective marketing strategies and improved user experiences.

Lastly, the integration of AI in creating customer profiles extends to personalised marketing strategies. With detailed customer insights, e-commerce platforms can craft targeted campaigns that resonate with specific segments. This level of personalisation can significantly enhance the effectiveness of marketing efforts, leading to higher engagement and conversion rates. AI tools can also assist in optimising pricing strategies, ensuring that offers are aligned with customer expectations and willingness to pay. By embracing AI-driven customer profiling, e-commerce businesses position themselves to thrive in a competitive landscape, ultimately leading to sustained growth and success.

Targeted Marketing Campaigns

Targeted marketing campaigns are essential for e-commerce businesses aiming to connect effectively with their consumer base. By leveraging the capabilities of artificial intelligence, these campaigns can be tailored to meet the specific needs and preferences of individual customers. This personalisation improves engagement and conversion rates, as consumers are more likely to respond to offers and products that align closely with their interests. AI-driven product recommendation systems are one of the most effective tools in enabling businesses to analyse customer behaviour and suggest products that are likely to resonate with each individual.

Integrating chatbots into customer service strategies enhances the effectiveness of targeted marketing campaigns. These AI-powered tools can engage with customers in real-time, providing tailored recommendations and support based on user inquiries and past interactions. This not only improves the customer experience but also allows businesses to gather valuable data on consumer preferences and behaviour. By analysing this information, e-commerce platforms can adjust their marketing strategies, ensuring that promotional efforts are directed toward the right audience segments at the right times, thus maximising impact.

Predictive analytics plays a crucial role in inventory management and targeted marketing. By utilising historical data and consumer trends, businesses can forecast demand for specific products, allowing them to adjust their marketing campaigns accordingly. This strategic alignment ensures that promotional efforts coincide with key buying periods, reducing the likelihood of stockouts or excess inventory.

Additionally, understanding which products are likely to be popular enables e-commerce platforms to craft targeted messages that highlight these items, further enhancing the effectiveness of their campaigns.

Personalised marketing strategies are at the heart of successful e-commerce initiatives. AI algorithms can analyse vast amounts of data to segment audiences based on various criteria, such as purchasing behaviour, demographics, and browsing history. With this segmentation, businesses can create highly targeted advertisements that speak directly to the interests and needs of each group. This level of personalisation not only increases the likelihood of conversion but also fosters brand loyalty, as consumers feel understood and valued by the business.

Finally, incorporating AI-based pricing optimisation tools into targeted marketing campaigns can significantly enhance profitability. By analysing market trends, competitor pricing, and consumer demand, these tools allow businesses to adjust their pricing strategies dynamically. This not only ensures that prices remain competitive but also enables e-commerce platforms to maximise revenue during peak sales periods. Ultimately, the combination of targeted marketing campaigns with advanced AI technologies provides a robust framework for e-commerce success, helping businesses to engage customers more effectively and drive sales growth.

Evaluating the Effectiveness of Personalised Marketing

Evaluating the effectiveness of personalised marketing is crucial for e-commerce businesses looking to leverage AI technologies to enhance customer engagement and drive sales. Personalised marketing refers to tailoring marketing efforts to individual customer preferences and behaviours, facilitated by data analysis and AI algorithms.

Understanding how to measure the success of these strategies can help e-commerce professionals identify which approaches yield the highest returns on investment, allowing them to optimise their marketing efforts effectively.

One key metric for evaluating personalised marketing effectiveness is conversion rates. By analysing the percentage of users who complete a desired action, such as making a purchase after receiving a personalised recommendation, businesses can gauge how well their marketing strategies align with customer needs. A higher conversion rate typically indicates that personalised content resonates with the target audience, highlighting the importance of using AI-driven product recommendation systems. These systems analyse user data to suggest relevant products, making the shopping experience more enjoyable and efficient, ultimately leading to increased sales.

Another important aspect of evaluating personalised marketing is customer retention. It is often more cost-effective to retain existing customers than to acquire new ones, and personalised marketing can play a significant role in fostering loyalty. By tracking repeat purchase rates and customer lifetime value, e-commerce businesses can assess how effective their personalised strategies are in encouraging long-term relationships with customers. Additionally, AI tools can analyse user behaviour to identify patterns, allowing businesses to refine their marketing tactics based on what drives customer loyalty.

Engagement metrics, such as click-through rates and time spent on site, also provide valuable insights into the effectiveness of personalised marketing campaigns.

Increased engagement often correlates with a positive user experience, which is essential in a competitive e-commerce landscape. AI-enhanced supply chain logistics and chatbot integration for customer service can further improve user experiences by providing quick and relevant responses to inquiries, thus enhancing the overall shopping journey. Evaluating these engagement metrics alongside conversion and retention rates enables businesses to develop a comprehensive understanding of their personalised marketing effectiveness.

Finally, it is essential to consider the role of predictive analytics in evaluating personalised marketing. By forecasting future customer behaviour based on historical data, businesses can adjust their marketing strategies proactively. This includes optimising pricing through AI-based pricing tools and ensuring that inventory management aligns with predicted demand. As e-commerce continues to evolve, the ability to harness AI for personalised marketing will be a critical factor in maintaining a competitive edge. By systematically evaluating these various aspects of personalised marketing, e-commerce professionals can refine their strategies and drive sustainable growth in their businesses.

Chapter 6

AI-Based Pricing Optimisation Tools

The Science Behind Pricing Strategies

The science behind pricing strategies is a critical area of study for anyone involved in e-commerce, as it directly impacts consumer behaviour and business profitability.

Pricing is not merely about assigning a number to a product; it involves understanding the psychological and economic principles that guide customer purchasing decisions. Various factors, such as perceived value, competition, and market demand, play a significant role in how prices are set and adjusted over time. Students and professionals must appreciate these dynamics to craft effective pricing strategies that resonate with their target audience.

One of the pivotal elements in pricing strategy is the concept of perceived value. This refers to the customer's evaluation of a product based on its benefits relative to its cost. E-commerce platforms can leverage AI-driven tools to analyse customer feedback and behaviour, helping businesses understand how consumers perceive value.

For instance, AI algorithms can assess reviews, ratings, and purchasing patterns to refine pricing models that align with customer expectations. This insight enables e-commerce businesses to maintain competitive pricing while enhancing customer satisfaction.

Competitive analysis is another crucial aspect of pricing strategy. E-commerce retailers must be aware of their competitors' pricing structures and strategies to remain relevant in the market. AI technologies can facilitate real-time pricing comparisons and market trend analysis, allowing businesses to adjust their prices dynamically. Such tools can help identify optimal price points that attract customers while ensuring profitability. By employing AI-driven pricing optimisation tools, e-commerce professionals can develop strategies that respond swiftly to market changes and consumer demand fluctuations.

Moreover, predictive analytics plays a vital role in inventory management, which is closely tied to pricing strategies. Understanding which products are likely to be in demand allows businesses to set prices that maximise revenue while minimising overstock or stockouts. AI can analyse historical sales data, seasonal trends, and external market factors to forecast inventory needs accurately. This foresight enables e-commerce businesses to establish pricing strategies that not only appeal to consumers but also align with their operational capacities, ensuring a balanced supply-demand equation.

Lastly, personalised marketing strategies using AI algorithms can significantly enhance pricing approaches. By analysing user behaviour, preferences, and past purchases, e-commerce platforms can create tailored pricing offers that appeal to individual customers. This level of personalisation not only improves customer engagement but also increases the likelihood of conversion. AI tools can help identify the optimal price points for targeted segments, allowing businesses to implement dynamic pricing models that adapt to changing consumer behaviours and market conditions.

Understanding these scientific principles behind pricing strategies equips e-commerce students and professionals with the knowledge needed to drive sales and improve overall business performance.

AI Tools for Dynamic Pricing

Dynamic pricing is an essential strategy for e-commerce businesses aiming to maximise revenue and stay competitive in an ever-evolving market. AI tools for dynamic pricing leverage vast amounts of data to adjust prices in real-time based on various factors such as demand fluctuations, competitor pricing, inventory levels, and even customer behaviour patterns. By employing sophisticated algorithms, these tools enable businesses to implement pricing strategies that are not only responsive but also tailored to individual customer segments, enhancing overall profitability.

One of the primary advantages of AI-driven dynamic pricing tools is their ability to analyse historical data alongside real-time market conditions. For instance, machine learning algorithms can identify trends from past sales data, predicting future demand for products. This predictive capability allows e-commerce professionals to make informed decisions about when to raise or lower prices, ensuring that they are optimising their sales potential while maintaining a competitive edge. Moreover, these tools can automatically adjust prices based on competitor actions, ensuring that businesses remain attractive to price-sensitive customers.

Incorporating AI into dynamic pricing also enhances personalised marketing strategies. By analysing user behaviour and purchase history, AI tools can suggest personalised pricing offers to individual customers, making them feel valued and more likely to complete a purchase. For example, if a customer frequently buys a specific type of product, an AI pricing tool may offer them a discount on their next purchase, thus fostering customer loyalty and encouraging repeat business. This level of personalisation can significantly improve the overall shopping experience while driving higher conversion rates.

The integration of AI tools for dynamic pricing extends beyond just pricing adjustments; it also plays a crucial role in inventory management. Predictive analytics can forecast stock levels based on anticipated demand, allowing e-commerce businesses to adjust prices accordingly. If inventory is running low, prices can be increased to maximise profit on remaining stock, while surplus inventory might necessitate price reductions to encourage sales. This strategic approach not only optimises revenue but also minimises the risk of excess stock, ultimately enhancing the efficiency of the supply chain.

Finally, the implementation of AI-driven dynamic pricing tools requires careful consideration of ethical implications and customer perceptions. Transparency in pricing strategies is vital to maintain customer trust, as sudden price fluctuations can lead to dissatisfaction. Educating customers about the rationale behind dynamic pricing, such as the benefits of personalised offers or the need to respond to market conditions, can help mitigate potential backlash. By fostering an understanding of how AI tools enhance their shopping experience, e-commerce businesses can leverage dynamic pricing as a strategic asset that aligns with both their revenue goals and customer satisfaction.

Case Studies on Pricing Optimisation

Case studies on pricing optimisation reveal how various e-commerce businesses have successfully leveraged AI-driven tools to enhance their pricing strategies. One notable example is an online fashion retailer that implemented an AI-based pricing optimisation tool. The tool analysed vast amounts of data, including competitor pricing, customer demand, and sales trends, allowing the retailer to adjust prices dynamically. As a result, the retailer saw a significant increase in conversion rates and overall revenue, demonstrating how intelligent pricing strategies can lead to improved market competitiveness.

Another compelling case study involves a leading electronics e-commerce platform that utilised predictive analytics to refine its pricing models. By integrating historical data and real-time sales information, the platform developed a pricing strategy that adjusted based on inventory levels and seasonal demand fluctuations. This approach not only helped in reducing overstock and markdowns but also improved customer satisfaction by ensuring competitive pricing. The platform reported a notable increase in customer loyalty, as consumers felt they were receiving fair prices based on market conditions.

In the realm of AI-enhanced supply chain logistics, a grocery e-commerce service adopted an AI-driven pricing optimisation tool that considered supply chain variables when setting prices. This service faced unique challenges, such as perishable goods and fluctuating demand. By employing AI algorithms, the platform was able to optimise pricing based on freshness, availability, and consumer buying patterns. The results were impressive, with a marked increase in sales of perishable items and reduced waste, highlighting the importance of integrating pricing strategies with supply chain considerations.

Further illustrating the potential of AI in pricing optimisation, a luxury goods e-commerce site used advanced machine learning algorithms to personalise pricing for individual customers. By analysing user behaviour and purchase history, the site tailored prices and promotions to fit the preferences of different consumer segments. This personalised approach not only boosted sales but also enhanced customer engagement, as users felt valued and understood. The case illustrates how AI can transform pricing from a one-size-fits-all model to a more nuanced strategy that caters to diverse customer needs.

Lastly, a subscription-based e-commerce model adopted AI-driven pricing optimisation to enhance customer retention and maximise lifetime value. The platform analysed customer usage patterns and adjusted subscription prices based on user engagement levels and perceived value. By offering tiered pricing options that aligned with user behaviour, the service successfully retained customers while increasing average revenue per user. This case study highlights the effectiveness of dynamic pricing strategies in subscription models and emphasises the role of AI in understanding and responding to customer needs in real time.

Chapter 7

AI-Enhanced Supply Chain Logistics

Understanding Supply Chain Challenges in E-commerce

The landscape of e-commerce has transformed dramatically over the past decade, largely driven by technological advancements. However, with this rapid evolution comes a host of supply chain challenges that e-commerce businesses must navigate. One of the most significant challenges is managing inventory effectively. Traditional inventory management systems often fall short in the dynamic environment of e-commerce, where demand can fluctuate rapidly due to factors like seasonality, promotions, or even viral trends. Understanding how to leverage AI-driven predictive analytics can help businesses anticipate demand, optimise stock levels, and reduce the risk of overstocking or stockouts.

Another critical challenge in the e-commerce supply chain is ensuring the timely delivery of products. With consumers increasingly expecting fast shipping options, businesses must develop efficient logistics strategies. AI-enhanced supply chain logistics tools can analyse data in real time to streamline operations, predict delivery times, and optimise routing for shipping. This capability not only improves customer satisfaction but also reduces operational costs. E-commerce professionals must familiarise themselves with these tools to effectively manage logistics and enhance their overall service delivery.

The integration of AI technologies in customer service also plays a pivotal role in addressing supply chain challenges. Chatbot integration provides a seamless way to handle customer inquiries regarding order status, shipping details, and return policies. These AI-driven solutions can operate around the clock, ensuring that customers receive timely responses and support, which ultimately fosters loyalty and trust. For e-commerce newcomers, understanding how to implement and utilise chatbots can significantly enhance the customer experience and alleviate the strain on human customer service representatives.

Personalisation has emerged as a key strategy in e-commerce marketing, yet it poses its own challenges within the supply chain context. Implementing personalised marketing strategies requires a deep understanding of user behaviour, which can be achieved through AI algorithms. By analysing customer data, businesses can tailor their offerings to meet individual preferences, thereby driving sales. However, this personalisation must align with supply chain capabilities to ensure that products are available when and where customers expect them. E-commerce professionals must strike a balance between personalisation and operational feasibility to ensure sustainable growth.

Lastly, pricing optimisation is another area where e-commerce businesses face supply chain challenges. AI-based pricing optimisation tools enable companies to dynamically adjust prices based on market demand, competitor pricing, and inventory levels.

However, these strategies require a robust understanding of the supply chain to avoid scenarios where rapid price changes affect stock availability or lead to customer dissatisfaction. E-commerce students and professionals should focus on integrating pricing strategies with supply chain management to create a cohesive approach that maximises profitability while maintaining a positive customer experience.

AI Solutions for Streamlining Logistics

In the evolving landscape of e-commerce, efficient logistics management is critical to success. Artificial intelligence offers a suite of solutions that can dramatically enhance logistics operations, enabling businesses to streamline processes, reduce costs, and improve customer satisfaction. One of the key areas where AI shines is in supply chain optimisation. By employing machine learning algorithms, e-commerce platforms can analyse vast amounts of data to forecast demand, optimise inventory levels, and ensure that products are available when and where customers want them.

Predictive analytics plays a vital role in inventory management, allowing companies to anticipate trends and fluctuations in consumer behaviour. By leveraging historical sales data, seasonal trends, and market conditions, AI-driven tools can help businesses make informed decisions about stock levels, reducing the risk of overstocking or stockouts. This not only enhances operational efficiency but also supports a more responsive and agile logistics framework, crucial for meeting customer expectations in a fast-paced online shopping environment.

AI also excels in enhancing supply chain visibility. Through real-time tracking and monitoring of shipments, businesses can gain insights into their logistics operations, identify potential bottlenecks, and respond proactively to delays. Machine learning algorithms can analyse this data to recommend optimal routes and transportation methods, minimising costs and maximising delivery speed. This level of transparency allows e-commerce companies to keep their customers informed about order status, thereby improving the overall shopping experience.

Chatbots and AI assistants are transforming customer service in logistics as well. By integrating these tools into their platforms, e-commerce businesses can provide immediate responses to customer inquiries about shipping, order tracking, and delivery times. This not only improves customer satisfaction but also frees up human resources to focus on more complex tasks. The ability of AI-driven chatbots to learn from interactions means they continuously improve their responses, offering a more personalised experience for users.

Finally, AI-based pricing optimisation tools are essential for balancing profitability and competitiveness in e-commerce logistics. By analysing market trends, competitor pricing, and consumer behaviour, these tools can recommend dynamic pricing strategies that adapt in real time to changes in the market. This capability ensures that e-commerce businesses can remain agile and responsive, making informed pricing decisions that align with their overall logistics and operational strategies. As AI continues to advance, its role in streamlining logistics will only become more integral to e-commerce success.

The Future of AI in Supply Chain Management

The future of artificial intelligence (AI) in supply chain management is poised to revolutionise how e-commerce businesses operate, offering unprecedented efficiency and adaptability. As e-commerce continues to grow, the complexities of managing supply chains will increase, necessitating innovative solutions. AI technologies, such as predictive

Smart Selling: Harnessing AI for E-commerce Success

analytics and machine learning algorithms, are already transforming traditional supply chain practices. These advancements enable businesses to anticipate demand fluctuations, optimise inventory levels, and streamline logistics, ensuring that products are delivered to customers in a timely manner.

One of the most significant impacts of AI in supply chain management is its ability to enhance inventory management through predictive analytics. By analysing historical sales data, seasonal trends, and external factors such as economic conditions, AI systems can forecast demand with remarkable accuracy. This capability allows e-commerce businesses to maintain optimal stock levels, reducing the risk of overstocking or stockouts. As a result, companies can minimise holding costs while improving customer satisfaction by ensuring that products are available when needed.

Additionally, AI-driven product recommendation systems are becoming increasingly sophisticated. These systems analyse user behaviour and preferences, enabling e-commerce platforms to tailor product suggestions to individual customers. By integrating these AI technologies into supply chain management, businesses can ensure that popular items are readily available, thereby enhancing the overall shopping experience. Personalised marketing strategies, powered by AI algorithms, further complement this approach by targeting specific customer segments with relevant promotions, leading to increased conversion rates and customer loyalty.

The integration of chatbots and AI assistants in customer service is another area where supply chain management is evolving. These intelligent systems can handle customer inquiries about product availability, order status, and delivery times, providing real-time information and support. This level of responsiveness not only improves customer satisfaction but also reduces the workload on human agents, allowing them to focus on more complex issues. As e-commerce businesses adopt these AI-driven solutions, they can create a more seamless and efficient interaction with their customers, fostering a stronger relationship and a better overall experience.

The future of AI in supply chain logistics is also bright, with advancements in AI-enhanced logistics solutions paving the way for smarter shipping and delivery methods. Companies are leveraging AI to optimise route planning, reduce transportation costs, and improve delivery times. Furthermore, the rise of voice commerce and AI assistants is reshaping online shopping experiences, enabling customers to place orders and manage their purchases through voice commands. As these technologies continue to advance, e-commerce businesses that harness the power of AI in their supply chain management will not only improve operational efficiency but also position themselves as leaders in a rapidly evolving market.

Chapter 8

Voice Commerce and AI Assistants

The Rise of Voice Commerce

The rise of voice commerce represents a significant shift in the way consumers interact with e-commerce platforms. As smart speakers and voice assistants like Amazon Alexa, Google Assistant, and Apple's Siri become increasingly integrated into daily life, the landscape of online shopping is evolving. This transformation is not just a trend; it reflects a fundamental change in consumer behaviour, where convenience and efficiency drive purchasing decisions. E-commerce students and professionals must understand how voice commerce can enhance the shopping experience and what implications it has for their business strategies.

Voice commerce offers distinct advantages that traditional e-commerce methods cannot match. The hands-free, fast, and intuitive nature of voice commands allows consumers to search for products, make purchases, and even track deliveries without the need for screens. This ease of use is particularly appealing in a fast-paced world where multitasking is common. As e-commerce businesses explore voice commerce, they should prioritise optimising their platforms for voice search, ensuring that their product listings are compatible with voice queries, enhancing discoverability, and improving user engagement.

AI-driven product recommendation systems are integral to the voice commerce experience. These systems analyse user behaviour and preferences to deliver tailored product suggestions during voice interactions. When a consumer asks a voice assistant for recommendations, the AI can leverage past purchase data and browsing history to provide personalised options, thereby increasing the likelihood of conversion. E-commerce professionals should focus on refining these algorithms to enhance the accuracy and relevance of the recommendations, creating a seamless shopping experience that resonates with consumers.

Incorporating chatbots and AI assistants into the voice commerce framework can further streamline customer service interactions. Chatbots are essential in voice commerce for handling inquiries, processing orders, and offering real-time support. By integrating natural language processing (NLP), these chatbots can understand and respond to a wide range of customer requests, enhancing the overall shopping experience. E-commerce businesses must invest in developing sophisticated chatbot technology that complements voice commerce, ensuring that customers receive timely and accurate support.

Predictive analytics plays a critical role in inventory management and supply chain logistics within the voice commerce realm. By analysing consumer data and purchasing trends, businesses can better anticipate demand, optimise stock levels, and reduce the risk of overstocking or stockouts. This strategic use of AI not only improves operational efficiency but also enhances the customer experience by ensuring that popular products are readily available for voice-activated purchases. As the voice commerce sector continues to grow, e-commerce professionals must embrace these technologies to remain competitive and meet the evolving needs of consumers.

Integrating AI Assistants into E-commerce Platforms

Integrating AI assistants into e-commerce platforms is a transformative step that redefines how businesses engage with customers and streamline operations. AI assistants, including chatbots and virtual shopping assistants, serve as vital tools that enhance customer service while providing personalised shopping experiences. By leveraging natural language processing and machine learning, these AI technologies can interpret customer inquiries, offer tailored product recommendations, and resolve issues in real time, ultimately improving customer satisfaction and retention.

One of the key applications of AI assistants is in the realm of product recommendation systems. These systems analyse user behaviour, preferences, and past purchases to suggest relevant products to customers, making the shopping experience more intuitive and engaging. By utilising algorithms that learn from user interactions, e-commerce platforms can deliver personalised suggestions that not only increase conversion rates but also enhance the overall shopping experience. This targeted approach helps businesses to stand out in a crowded marketplace, as customers feel understood and valued.

In addition to enhancing customer interactions, AI assistants play a crucial role in inventory management through predictive analytics. By forecasting demand based on historical data and current trends, these tools can help e-commerce businesses optimise their inventory levels, reducing overhead costs and minimising stockouts or overstock situations. This proactive management ensures that customers find the products they want when they want them, further solidifying their trust and loyalty to the brand.

Personalised marketing strategies powered by AI-driven algorithms also benefit significantly from the integration of AI assistants. These systems can analyse extensive datasets to segment audiences effectively and tailor marketing messages that resonate with specific groups. By understanding customer behaviour and preferences, businesses can craft promotions and advertisements that are not only relevant but also timely, leading to increased engagement and sales. This level of personalisation is crucial for maintaining competitiveness in the fast-evolving e-commerce landscape.

Lastly, the integration of voice commerce with AI assistants marks a new frontier in online shopping experiences. As consumers increasingly utilise voice-activated devices for their shopping needs, e-commerce platforms must adapt by incorporating voice recognition capabilities into their AI systems. This integration allows for seamless transactions and enhances user experience, as customers can browse, compare, and purchase products using simple voice commands. By embracing this innovative technology, e-commerce businesses can meet the expectations of modern consumers who seek convenience and efficiency in their shopping journeys.

Enhancing User Experience Through Voice Interaction

Voice interaction is rapidly transforming the landscape of e-commerce, providing an innovative approach to enhance user experience. As consumers increasingly adopt voice-activated devices, businesses must adapt to this trend to remain competitive. By integrating voice interaction into e-commerce platforms, companies can create a more engaging and intuitive shopping experience. This approach allows customers to interact with online stores in a conversational manner, simplifying the process of finding products, making purchases, and receiving support. The convenience and speed of voice commands can significantly reduce friction in the shopping journey, leading to higher customer satisfaction and loyalty.

Smart Selling: Harnessing AI for E-commerce Success

Implementing voice interaction tools requires a strategic understanding of customer preferences and behaviour. E-commerce businesses can utilise AI-driven product recommendation systems to tailor voice responses according to user profiles and past interactions. By analysing user data, these systems can suggest relevant products or promotions, thereby creating a personalised shopping experience. For instance, when a customer asks for recommendations based on their previous purchases, the AI can provide tailored suggestions that are more likely to convert into sales. This level of personalisation not only boosts engagement but also reinforces the customer's relationship with the brand.

In addition to enhancing product discovery, voice interaction can significantly improve customer service in online retail. Chatbot integration, powered by AI, allows businesses to handle inquiries and issues through voice commands, providing instant responses to common questions. This capability can decrease wait times and enhance user satisfaction, as customers receive immediate assistance without navigating through complicated menus or waiting for human agents. Furthermore, voice-activated chatbots can operate around the clock, ensuring that support is always readily available, which is particularly important for e-commerce platforms with a global customer base.

Predictive analytics further complements voice interaction by optimising inventory management and marketing strategies. By understanding user behaviour through voice commands, e-commerce platforms can identify trends and make data-driven decisions regarding stock levels and product offerings. For example, if voice searches reveal a growing interest in a specific product category, businesses can adjust their inventory accordingly. Additionally, AI algorithms can analyse the data collected from voice interactions to refine personalised marketing efforts, ensuring that promotions resonate with the target audience and drive higher conversion rates.

Finally, as voice commerce continues to grow, companies must consider the broader implications for supply chain logistics and pricing strategies. AI-based tools can optimise pricing based on voice-activated user behaviour and market trends, allowing for dynamic adjustments that reflect real-time demand. This responsiveness can enhance competitiveness in the e-commerce space. Additionally, AI-enhanced supply chain logistics can streamline operations, ensuring that products are readily available to fulfil voice-activated orders efficiently. By embracing voice interaction and integrating it seamlessly with various AI-driven tools, e-commerce businesses can create a cohesive and enriched user experience that meets the evolving expectations of modern consumers.

Chapter 9

User Behaviour Analysis Using AI

Techniques for Analysing User Behaviour

Understanding user behaviour is essential for optimising e-commerce strategies, and employing various analytical techniques can significantly enhance this understanding. One of the foundational methods is tracking user interactions on e-commerce platforms through web analytics tools. These tools gather data on how users navigate through websites, including page visits, time spent on each page, and conversion rates. By analysing this data, e-commerce professionals can identify which areas of the site are performing well and which require improvement. This insight allows businesses to create more engaging user experiences, ensuring that potential buyers find what they need quickly, efficiently and with ease.

Another technique involves utilising AI-driven product recommendation systems that analyse user preferences and purchasing history. By employing machine learning algorithms, these systems can predict what products users are likely to buy based on their past behaviour and the behaviour of similar users. This personalised approach not only enhances the user experience but also drives sales by presenting customers with relevant options, thereby increasing the likelihood of conversions. Understanding the intricacies of these algorithms enables e-commerce professionals to refine their recommendation strategies, tailoring them to specific user segments for maximum effectiveness.

Chatbot integration in e-commerce platforms provides another layer of user behaviour analysis. These AI-powered tools engage with customers in real-time, answering queries and guiding them through the purchasing process. By analysing interactions and feedback from chatbots, businesses can gain valuable insights into common customer questions and concerns. This data can drive improvements in product descriptions, website navigation, and customer service strategies, ultimately leading to a more seamless shopping experience. Moreover, understanding user sentiment through chatbot interactions can inform broader marketing strategies and improve overall customer satisfaction.

Predictive analytics further enriches the analysis of user behaviour by forecasting future trends based on historical data. E-commerce businesses can utilise predictive models to anticipate inventory needs, ensuring that popular products are always available when customers seek them. By analysing patterns in user behaviour, businesses can optimise stock levels and reduce the risk of overstocking or stockouts. This technique not only streamlines operations but also enhances the customer experience, as users are more likely to find the products they want when they want them.

Lastly, AI-enhanced supply chain logistics plays a crucial role in understanding user behaviour by ensuring that products are delivered efficiently and promptly. By analysing user purchasing patterns and delivery preferences, e-commerce platforms can refine their logistics strategies, optimising routes and delivery times. This not only improves customer satisfaction but also reduces operational costs. As students and professionals in the e-commerce field explore these techniques, they will find that integrating various analytical methods can significantly enhance their understanding of user behaviour, leading to smarter, data-driven decisions that drive success in the competitive online retail landscape.

Tools for Enhancing E-commerce UX Design

In the rapidly evolving landscape of e-commerce, enhancing user experience (UX) design has become a pivotal focus for businesses striving to gain a competitive edge. Various tools and technologies have emerged that leverage artificial intelligence (AI) to streamline processes and optimise user interactions. The integration of AI-driven product recommendation systems serves as a prime example of how personalised experiences can significantly influence consumer behaviour. By analysing user data and preferences, these systems can suggest products that align closely with individual tastes, thereby increasing conversion rates and customer satisfaction.

Another essential tool in enhancing e-commerce UX is the deployment of chatbots for customer service. These AI-powered assistants provide immediate responses to customer inquiries, facilitating a seamless shopping experience. By understanding user queries through natural language processing, chatbots can resolve issues, provide product information, and even assist in the checkout process. Their 24/7 availability not only enhances customer engagement but also frees up human resources to focus on more complex inquiries, thereby improving overall service efficiency.

Predictive analytics is another vital component in optimising inventory management within e-commerce platforms. By leveraging AI algorithms to analyse historical sales data and market trends, businesses can forecast demand with greater accuracy. This capability enables retailers to maintain optimal inventory levels, preventing both overstock and stockouts, which can negatively impact the user experience. By ensuring that popular products are readily available, businesses can enhance customer satisfaction and loyalty, ultimately driving sales growth.

Personalised marketing strategies powered by AI algorithms further amplify the impact of UX design in e-commerce. Through the analysis of user behaviour and preferences, businesses can tailor marketing messages and promotions to resonate with individual customers. This level of customisation not only increases the relevance of marketing efforts but also fosters a deeper connection between the brand and its audience. By presenting users with content that aligns with their interests, e-commerce platforms can significantly improve engagement rates and conversion potential.

Lastly, the integration of AI-based pricing optimisation tools is critical for maintaining competitiveness in the e-commerce sector. These tools analyse market dynamics, competitor pricing, and consumer behaviour to recommend optimal pricing strategies that maximise profitability while remaining attractive to customers. Additionally, AI-enhanced supply chain logistics can streamline operations, ensuring products are delivered efficiently and on time, which is paramount to user satisfaction. As e-commerce continues to evolve, embracing these innovative tools will be essential for students, novices, and professionals alike to create compelling and user-friendly online shopping experiences.

Leveraging Data for Continuous Improvement

Leveraging data effectively is crucial for continuous improvement in e-commerce, especially as the landscape rapidly evolves with technology. By harnessing the power of data analytics, e-commerce businesses can gain valuable insights into customer behaviour, preferences, and market trends. This understanding allows companies to make informed decisions that enhance their operations and improve customer experiences. From AI-driven product recommendation systems to personalised marketing strategies, utilising data can significantly boost sales and customer engagement.

Smart Selling: Harnessing AI for E-commerce Success

AI-driven product recommendation systems exemplify how data can enhance the shopping experience. By analysing past purchases, browsing history, and user preferences, these systems can suggest products that are more likely to resonate with individual customers. This not only increases the likelihood of additional sales but also fosters a sense of personalisation that can lead to increased customer loyalty. E-commerce platforms that leverage such technology can more effectively meet customer needs and demands, adapting their offerings in real-time based on data insights.

Incorporating chatbots into customer service is another area where data can drive continuous improvement. These AI-powered tools can analyse customer queries and behaviours to provide immediate, relevant responses. By monitoring interactions and identifying common questions or issues, businesses can refine their chatbots to enhance user satisfaction. Furthermore, the data collected from these interactions can inform broader customer service strategies, allowing businesses to address pain points and streamline processes based on real user feedback.

Predictive analytics plays a vital role in inventory management for e-commerce businesses. By leveraging historical sales data and market trends, companies can forecast demand more accurately, reducing the risk of overstocking or stockouts. This data-driven approach enables businesses to optimise their supply chain logistics, ensuring that products are available when customers want them without incurring unnecessary costs. Continuous monitoring and analysis of this data can help businesses adjust their strategies dynamically, responding swiftly to changes in consumer demand.

Personalised marketing strategies are another area where data can be leveraged for continuous improvement. By utilising AI algorithms to segment customers based on their behaviours and preferences, e-commerce businesses can create targeted marketing campaigns that resonate with specific audiences. These tailored approaches not only increase conversion rates but also enhance the overall shopping experience. As businesses gather more data on customer interactions and preferences, they can refine their marketing strategies further, fostering deeper connections with their audience and driving long-term success in the competitive e-commerce landscape.

Chapter 10

Future Trends in AI and E-commerce

Emerging Technologies to Watch

Emerging technologies are reshaping the landscape of e-commerce, bringing forth innovative solutions that can significantly enhance business operations and customer experience. One of the most promising advancements lies in AI-driven product recommendation systems. These systems analyse user behaviour, preferences, and purchase history to suggest products that are most likely to resonate with individual customers. By leveraging machine learning algorithms, e-commerce platforms can provide tailored recommendations that not only boost sales but also foster customer loyalty. As students and professionals venture into the e-commerce space, understanding how to implement and optimise these systems will be crucial for driving engagement and conversions.

In addition to product recommendations, chatbot integration is revolutionising customer service in the online retail sector. These AI-powered assistants can handle a wide range of inquiries, from product availability to order tracking, thus providing instant support to customers around the clock. The implementation of chatbots can lead to improved customer satisfaction, reduced operational costs, and enhanced efficiency in handling queries. As aspiring e-commerce professionals, learning how to design and integrate effective chatbot solutions will be essential in creating seamless customer interactions and managing service demands.

Predictive analytics is another vital technology that is transforming inventory management in e-commerce. By analysing historical sales data and market trends, predictive analytics tools enable businesses to forecast demand, optimise stock levels, and minimise excess inventory. This data-driven approach ensures that e-commerce platforms can maintain the right amount of stock, thereby reducing costs and enhancing customer satisfaction through timely product availability. As e-commerce students, mastering predictive analytics will empower you to make informed decisions that positively impact overall business performance.

Personalised marketing strategies powered by AI algorithms are also gaining momentum in the e-commerce landscape. Utilising customer data, these strategies allow businesses to create targeted marketing campaigns that resonate with specific audience segments. By tailoring promotions and communication to individual preferences, e-commerce platforms can enhance engagement and increase conversion rates. Understanding how to harness AI for personalised marketing will equip new professionals with the skills needed to effectively reach and retain customers in a competitive environment.

Lastly, the rise of voice commerce and AI assistants is shaping the future of online shopping experiences. As more consumers adopt voice-activated devices, integrating voice commerce capabilities into e-commerce platforms can provide a hands-free shopping experience that appeals to modern consumers. Coupled with user behaviour analysis using AI, businesses can refine their e-commerce user experience UX design to create intuitive and engaging interfaces. Embracing these technologies will allow new entrants in the e-commerce field to stay ahead of trends and deliver exceptional shopping experiences that meet the evolving needs of consumers.

The Impact of AI on E-commerce Strategies

The integration of artificial intelligence (AI) into e-commerce strategies has revolutionised the way businesses operate, offering unprecedented opportunities for efficiency and personalisation. For students and professionals in the e-commerce space, understanding how AI influences various aspects of online retail is crucial for developing effective strategies. AI-driven product recommendation systems, for instance, utilise vast amounts of consumer data to suggest products tailored to individual preferences. This not only enhances user experience but also increases conversion rates, as shoppers are more likely to purchase items that align with their interests.

Another significant impact of AI in e-commerce is the deployment of chatbots for customer service. These AI-powered tools provide immediate assistance to customers, addressing common inquiries and resolving issues without human intervention. By analysing user interactions and feedback, chatbots continuously improve their responses, leading to enhanced customer satisfaction. For e-commerce professionals, integrating chatbots into their customer service framework can lead to reduced operational costs and improved response times, creating a more streamlined shopping experience.

Predictive analytics is another area where AI is making strides, particularly in inventory management. By analysing historical sales data, seasonal trends, and consumer behaviour patterns, predictive analytics tools can forecast demand with greater accuracy. This capability enables e-commerce businesses to optimise their inventory levels, ensuring that they meet customer demand without overstocking. For students and newcomers to the e-commerce field, mastering these predictive tools is essential for maintaining an efficient supply chain and minimising costs associated with excess inventory.

Personalised marketing strategies powered by AI algorithms are transforming how e-commerce businesses engage with their customers. By leveraging data on user behaviour and preferences, companies can create targeted marketing campaigns that resonate with specific audience segments. This level of personalisation not only enhances customer engagement but also fosters brand loyalty. As professionals delve into the intricacies of e-commerce marketing, understanding the role of AI in crafting personalised experiences will be a key differentiator in a competitive landscape.

Additionally, AI-based pricing optimisation tools are becoming indispensable for e-commerce businesses aiming to maximise profitability. These tools analyse market trends, competitor pricing, and consumer demand to suggest optimal pricing strategies. By adopting such technologies, e-commerce professionals can remain agile and responsive to market shifts, ensuring that their pricing remains competitive while also reflecting the perceived value of their products. As e-commerce continues to evolve, the ability to harness AI for pricing strategies will be vital for sustained success in the digital marketplace.

Preparing for the Future of Retail with AI

Preparing for the future of retail with AI involves an understanding of various AI technologies and their applications in the e-commerce sector. As the landscape of shopping evolves, e-commerce students and professionals must recognise the importance of AI-driven solutions in enhancing customer experiences, optimising operations, and driving sales. This preparation begins with familiarising oneself with AI tools that can transform traditional retail methods into more efficient, data-driven practices. By integrating AI solutions, businesses can not only streamline processes but also gain valuable insights into consumer behaviour, leading to more informed decision-making.

One of the most significant areas where AI is making an impact is in product recommendation systems. These systems leverage machine learning algorithms to analyse user behaviour and preferences, allowing e-commerce platforms to offer personalised product suggestions. This level of personalisation enhances the shopping experience by making it easier for customers to discover items that match their interests. E-commerce professionals should focus on implementing these systems effectively to boost conversion rates and customer satisfaction.

Understanding how these algorithms work and how to interpret their data can provide a competitive edge in the increasingly crowded and saturated online marketplace.

Chatbot integration is another critical component of AI in retail. Chatbots can handle customer inquiries, provide product information, and assist with order tracking, all while operating 24/7 (365 days a year). For e-commerce newcomers, mastering chatbot technology can significantly improve customer service and reduce operational costs. By utilising natural language processing, these AI-driven assistants can engage customers in meaningful conversations, enhancing their overall experience. E-commerce students should explore various chatbot frameworks and best practices to ensure they implement solutions that resonate with their target audience.

Predictive analytics plays a vital role in inventory management, helping e-commerce businesses forecast demand accurately and optimise stock levels. By analysing historical sales data and current market trends, AI can predict which products are likely to be in demand and when. This capability enables businesses to reduce overstock and stockouts, ultimately improving profitability. Aspiring e-commerce professionals must develop skills in data analysis and familiarise themselves with predictive tools to ensure they can effectively manage inventory and respond to market fluctuations.

Lastly, the future of retail will heavily rely on personalised marketing strategies powered by AI algorithms. These strategies analyse customer data to craft tailored marketing campaigns that resonate with individual consumers. E-commerce businesses that harness the power of AI for pricing optimisation and supply chain logistics can gain substantial advantages. As voice commerce and AI assistants become more integrated into online shopping experiences, understanding user behaviour through data analysis will be essential to enhance user experience UX design. E-commerce students and professionals should prioritise learning about these innovative technologies to prepare for a future where AI-driven solutions are at the forefront of retail success.